World Issues

FOOD TECHNOLOGY

Clive Gifford

Chrysalis Children's Books

WORLD ISSUES

ABORTION
ANIMAL RIGHTS
ARMS TRADE
CAPITAL PUNISHMENT
CONSUMERISM
DRUGS

EQUAL OPPORTUNITIES
EUTHANASIA
FOOD TECHNOLOGY
GENETIC ENGINEERING
GENOCIDE

HUMAN RIGHTS
POVERTY
RACISM
REFUGEES
TERRORISM

First published in the UK in 2004 by
(🌢) Chrysalis Children's Books
An imprint of Chrysalis Books Group plc
The Chrysalis Building, Bramley Road, London W10 6SP

Produced by Tall Tree Ltd

Editorial Manager: Joyce Bentley
Editor: Clare Lewis
Project Editor: Jon Richards
Designer: Ben Ruocco
Picture Researcher: Lorna Ainger
Educational consultant: Lizzy Bacon

ISBN: 1 84458 077 6

British Library Cataloguing in Publication Data for this book is available from
the British Library.
Printed in Hong Kong

10 9 8 7 6 5 4 3 2 1

Picture Acknowledgments
The publishers would like to thank the following for their permission to reproduce the photographs:
AKG, London: 13
Alamy Images: 48, C.N.R.I. 26, Nigel Cattlin 35, Foodfolio 18, G.Herbst 7, 45, Ansell Horn 31, Karen
Robinson 40, David Young-Wolff 47
Robert Battersby/Tografox: 11, 29, 32
Anthony Blake Photo Library: 12
Corbis: Bettmann 15, 17, 22, John B. Boykin 33, Patrik Giardino 44, Ray Krantz 14, Don Mason 34,
Liba Taylor 41
Getty Images: Tim Boyle 25, Piotr Malecki 9t, Spencer Platt 24, Joe Raedle 19
Holt Studios International: 5, 9b, 21, 36, 38
PA Photos: EPA 9c, 39, 43, 49, Fiona Hanson 46
Jon Richards 16
Science Photo Library: George Bernard 20, Mark Clarke 27, Mark Thomas 28
Still Pictures: Martha Cooper 42, M&C Denis-Huot 8, Jeff Greenberg 23, Robert Holmgren 37,
Thomas Meyer 10, Peter Schickert 30, Sean Sprague 50

CONTENTS

Joseph's Story

Joseph Maloba is a farmer in the highlands of Kenya. For the last ten years, he has supplied a Western food company with green beans and has become dependant upon their business. The company now says that the beans Joseph grows do not match their standards and has withdrawn their order, leaving Joseph to face financial ruin.

'MY NAME IS Joseph Maloba. My family has owned farmlands in the highlands of Kenya for many generations. In the past we grew many different crops which we sold in local markets but farming has changed greatly. About 40 or 50 years ago, 50 per cent of the money spent on food went to farmers, today that figure is much less than ten per cent.

Ten years ago, the company who bought most of my crop came to me with a contract. They told me they wanted my lands to grow just fine beans and insisted I used certain fertilisers and pesticides which were expensive for me to buy.

They also wanted me to guarantee that I would supply so many tonnes of the crop or face penalties. I had no choice but to sign the contract and they loaned me money for the expensive chemicals. Two years ago, I was told that my beans were no longer suitable. I could not understand it. They were healthy and tasted good. The company said they did not match their new standards – they had to be between 90 and 100 mm in length, 6–8mm in diameter and straight, not curved. The variety I grew was curved. These did not fit their packaging for European supermarkets. My crop was rejected and I had to sell many tonnes as livestock feed at a very low price. I am still paying back money to the company and I am deep in debt. I am fearful of genetically modified (GM) crops but it may be the only way that I can farm my lands again. One company has offered me GM seed for free for one growing season but only if I promise to buy their seed for many seasons to come.

Many members of my family work at a processing plant preparing baby vegetables and tying them into small bundles with straw for shops in Europe. The hours are long and they are exhausted, standing on their feet all day. They are picked up by the company bus at sunrise and sometimes do not get home until midnight. They have to prepare over 150 kg of vegetables each day for which they get paid 220 Kenyan shillings (around £1.70). When I hear that a pack of these fancy vegetables sells for as much as what a worker earns in a day here, I am filled with anger and upset. How can this be right?'

Food Technology across the world

Today, food technology is creating issues previously unconsidered in the wake of new processes.

USA
In the United States during 2001, 639 different food products were recalled from store shelves. Many of these products contained undeclared substances which were capable of causing dangerous allergic reactions in some people.

JAPAN
The worst outbreak of food poisoning in Japan for more than 30 years occurred in the Japanese city of Osaka in 2000. Some 14 500 people were victims of food poisoning traced to a batch of milk from the food company, Snow Brand, one of the world's 30 largest food companies.

EUROPE
Despite fears and opposition especially in Europe and the UK, genetically modified crops are being grown in increasingly large numbers around the world. In 2002, GM crops covered 58 million hectares worldwide – an area two and a half times the size of the UK.

What Is Food Technology?

Every time you open a can of beans, reach into a deep freezer for an ice cream or buy a pre-cooked pizza to be heated in a microwave oven, you are experiencing food technology in action. Food technology is the application of science and technology to create food products, to distribute them to stores and outlets and to help sell them to consumers.

OUR PLANET SUPPORTS an incredible array of different species of living things. Over a period of thousands of years, humankind discovered that many species were edible and could be hunted and caught, plucked from trees or dug out of the soil and eaten in order for people to survive and flourish. Today, few foods are eaten as they occur in the wild. Most foods which reach the plates of people, especially those in more developed nations such as in Europe and the USA, have been prepared and processed using food technology.

What is the difference between food science and food technology?

Food science is the discipline in which biology, chemistry, physics and engineering are all used to study the nature of foods.

Food science looks at why foods deteriorate or spoil over time, how foods can be mixed and altered to create different food products and how they can be preserved so that they last longer without spoiling and becoming unfit for us to eat. Food technology applies food science in practical ways to select foods, to process and preserve them and to distribute them to customers.

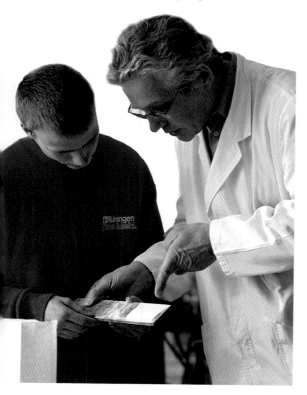

Today, food science and food technology are taught in universities and colleges around the world.

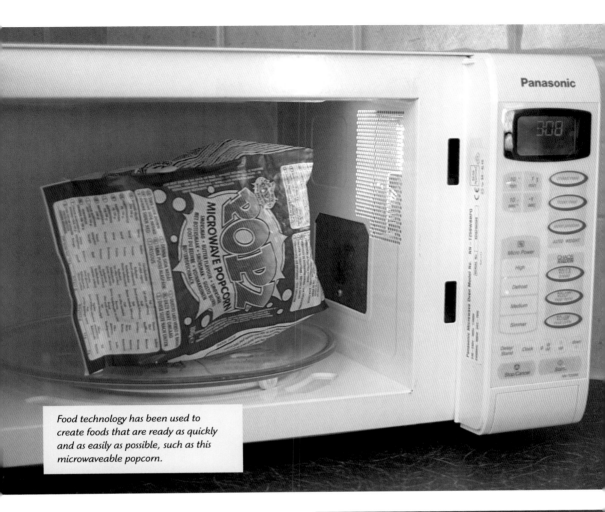

Food technology has been used to create foods that are ready as quickly and as easily as possible, such as this microwaveable popcorn.

Is food technology only about producing ready meals?

Food technology is more obviously at work in highly processed and packaged foods such as a ready meal, yet it also affects almost all of the food we eat. A strawberry you buy from a store may look as if it has not been touched by technology, but the truth is different. Food technology may have been involved in many stages; from how the fruit was grown, harvested, transported and packaged to the possibility that it was treated with radiation (see page 20–21) to increase the length of time it remains good to eat.

Revolutions in food

'In the last century nothing short of a revolution has taken place in the world of food. Every step along the chain – how it is grown, processed, distributed, retailed and cooked – has been transformed beyond recognition.'

Source: Tim Lang, Professor of Food Policy, City University, London

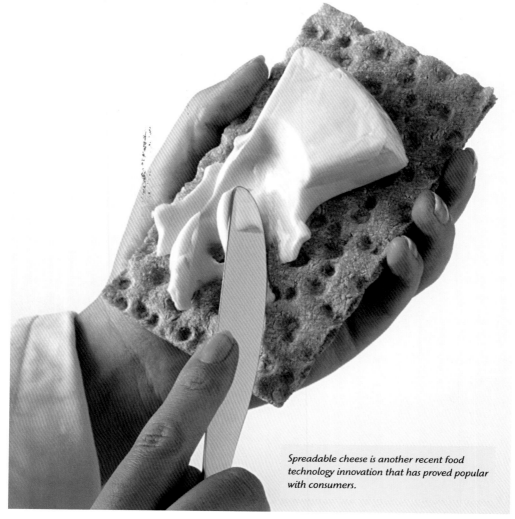

Spreadable cheese is another recent food technology innovation that has proved popular with consumers.

How does food technology work?

Cheese is sometimes used as an example of some of the many different ways food technology works. For a start, cheese is an example of a new food product. It does not occur naturally, but is the result of a series of human-made processes. Food technology often develops many versions of a food through altering ingredients and how the food is produced. Cheese is no different, with over 2000 different types.

Much of food technology's work is concerned with keeping foods from spoiling or going off. Many cheeses are sold in sealed plastic packs stored in supermarket chiller cabinets. Cheeses are often made from milk which has been pasteurised (see page 15) to kill bacteria and also contain substances which prolong their shelf life. Cheese has also been processed into new forms designed to be novel, easy to use and to excite the consumer into buying them. The arrival of processed cheese slices and cream cheese in a tube are examples of this aspect of food technology.

When was food technology first used?

Tens of thousands of years ago, humans survived usually by wandering from place to place in order to hunt animals, catch fish and gather foods from plants.

From around 8000 BC onwards, some peoples started to settle in one place and grow plants and rear livestock. The beginnings of food technology can be traced to this time in two different ways. Firstly, early farmers started to note which individual plants produced the largest crop or yield. By finding and saving these plants' seeds to sow the following year, farmers began to gain bigger harvests. Over many generations of selecting plants in this way, crop plants began to differ from their wild ancestors. Secondly, historians believe that wheat was one of the very first crops grown. Wheat grains are not very appetising but primitive food technology saw wheat grains crushed under stones to form a flour with which to bake bread. Over time, people discovered how yeasts – a range of

micro-organisms – could be added to bread to make it rise. Yeasts could also create alcohol from sugars and starches in fermentation – one of the first food technology processes to be developed. Beer-making is believed to have been practised at least as long as 5500 years ago in the Middle East.

This clay model depicts a bread-making scene from ancient Egypt dating back nearly 4000 years.

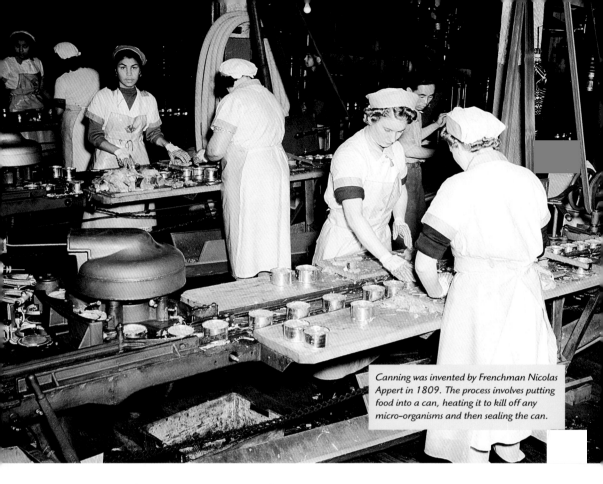

Canning was invented by Frenchman Nicolas Appert in 1809. The process involves putting food into a can, heating it to kill off any micro-organisms and then sealing the can.

How has food technology developed?

In the past 150 years, advances in science, technology, a huge increase in the world population and the rise of mass production in factories have all helped lead to more and more food technology innovations. The use of automated machinery in increasingly large factories has led to many foods being processed and produced in vast quantities. Plastics technology has developed to produce new ways of packaging goods. Canning, which stems from the early 19th century, and the rapid freezing process which was first introduced in the 1920s, enabled foods which perished quickly, such as fresh meat, fish and vegetables, to be transported around the world.
New foods have been created from

scratch while new uses and ways of eating age-old foodstuffs have been developed. One example of this is wheat and other cereal crops. Grown for thousands of years, crops like maize and wheat were first processed in the United States in the late 19th century into breakfast cereals. These products are now eaten by hundreds of millions of people every day.

Who invented frozen foods?

The American Clarence Birdseye (1886–1956) invented a quick freeze process in the 1920s. Working as a field naturalist in the Arctic, Birdseye saw at first hand how freezing freshly caught seafood kept its taste and texture when it was thawed out and eaten several weeks later. Setting up his first company in a

Pasteurisation

The French chemist, Louis Pasteur devised the process of pasteurisation in the 1860s. Pasteurisation involves heating a liquid such as milk, wine or fruit juice to a relatively high temperature, rapidly cooling it and then storing it below 10°C. Pasteurisation helps to sterilise substances such as milk by killing off micro-organisms called bacteria, some of which are potentially harmful.

New York fish market in 1922, Birdseye first froze seafood and then moved on to freeze meats, fruits and vegetables. For people living far from the coast or farming areas, rapid freezing increased the availability of foods such as fish and vegetables. However, if vegetables are frozen directly, substances called enzymes which are found in the vegetables tend to cause a slow deterioration in colour and flavour, even at low temperatures. To prevent this, most vegetables are blanched (immersed in very hot water or steam) before they are frozen. This action destroys the activity of the enzymes.

Has Food Technology Brought Benefits?

The world population has doubled in the last 50 years and increased ten times in the past three centuries. Great changes in farming and food technology have seen vast increases in the amount of food produced. Food technology has helped reduce food losses to spoilage and waste in harvesting and transportation. Despite criticisms and concerns, food technology has also brought a range of benefits to many people, including increased choice, greater convenience and lower prices.

Today, ready meals offer a wide range of menus, including many foreign or exotic foods, which can be ready in a matter of minutes.

OVER A CENTURY ago, typhoid, tuberculosis and cholera were diseases frequently transmitted through unsafe food and drink. Advances in food technology, such as the pasteurisation of milk and hygienic canning processes, have led to improvements in food safety which have helped conquer these diseases in many countries. Critics point out that other food-borne diseases remain, some of which may increasingly occur due to food technology practices.

How has food technology saved people time?

Food technology has slashed the time people have to spend shopping for, preparing and cooking food. In the past, most foods were perishable and had to be bought on an almost daily basis. Today, people can choose to shop far less regularly, relying on food stored in tins, dried packets or in frozen form. Many foods are sold already prepared so that much of the kitchen work has already been performed in food factories. Convenience foods and ready meals, which only need re-heating in an oven or microwave, have become a major part of people's diets. A survey in 2002 reported in the *Guardian* newspaper showed that teenagers in the UK eat an average of 133 of these convenience meals a year.

People today are looking to save money as well as time, and cheap, processed foods have helped to reduce the burden of the weekly food budget. Fifty years ago, people in more developed nations spent a third of their household income on food. Today, that figure has slipped to just a tenth of the household income.

This disturbing illustration shows the dangers of poor food hygiene throughout the 18th and 19th centuries. It was responsible for the spread of many deadly diseases during the period, including cholera.

According to a 2003 report, the typical supermarket stocks 35 000 different items, much of it in a wide range of tinned food, such as baked beans.

Global food

'Food has gone global. A green bean can now be growing in African soil one day and tossed into your supermarket trolley three days later. Advances in computer technology and communications have combined with dramatic falls in the cost of transport to transform the way we source our food.'

Source: Felicity Lawrence, *Why We Eat This Way*, *Guardian* newspaper

How has food technology increased choice?

Food technology has increased the number and range of food products available to people in the more developed nations of the world. Food processing and preservation techniques such as canning and freezing have made many foods available all year round which otherwise would only be on sale when in season. A century ago, few people in the UK would have eaten king prawns from the Pacific Ocean while few Americans would have tasted certain foods from the Indian subcontinent. Today, transport and improved storage technologies mean that foods can now go on sale which were originally grown or produced on the other side of the world.

Food technology has enabled foods and cuisines from different regions of the world to be packaged, promoted and sold to consumers in Europe and the United States. In the UK, for example, there has been a great increase in the number of Chinese, Thai and other Southeast Asian food products for sale in supermarkets. Hundreds of food products from Italy and the other nations found in the Mediterranean region have also been produced to fill supermarket shelves in the United States and the UK.

Many products that we take for granted today – from dried pasta in sauces to baked beans and ice cream – are the results of food technology and its ability to create new products. For example, Quorn, made from growing and processing a fungus, is one of a number of new meat-free foods, including tofu and soya, that are now available to people. First sold as the filling in savoury pies in 1985 after a ten year testing programme, Quorn is high in protein but low in calories, contains no cholesterol and has a third less fat than a skinless chicken breast.

DEBATE – Is more choice necessary?

- Yes. More new products give consumers more choice. Choice is a good thing and surveys show people like having a range of products to choose from.
- No. There is already far too much choice which is confusing to the consumer and wasteful. Every year, an estimated 13 000 new products are launched in the USA and around 10 000 in Europe. Over 85 per cent of these products fail in their first year on the shelves. Food companies would be better off spending the money on improving food safety than trying to create more products.

Quorn is now available to buy in a whole range of products, including burgers, sausages and ready meals.

The technical term for freeze-drying which created these coffee granules is lyophilisation.

How has food technology made food last longer?

All plants and animals naturally start to chemically change and deteriorate after they have been harvested or killed. Food technology has developed many ways of slowing or stalling the spoiling process and keeping bacteria and other spoiling agents at bay. Preserving methods and techniques include deep-freezing and pasteurisation looked at in the previous chapter. Other techniques include canning foods or vacuum-sealing foods in plastic packaging so that oxygen in air cannot reach the food product and cause spoiling reactions.

Why are many foods dried or freeze-dried?

Bacteria require water which is present in most foods when they are fresh. Drying food products to deny bacteria the water they need is thought to be the oldest food preservation technique of all, stretching back thousands of years. Many foodstuffs today, from pasta and fruit to herbs and rice, are dried. This not only helps preserve the food but also reduces its weight and makes many foods easier to transport without damaging them. However, drying rarely kills bacteria; it just prevents them from growing. As soon as the dried food absorbs water again, the bacteria can multiply and the food has to be treated with care. Freeze-drying is a process in which foods are frozen and then held in a vacuum as the ice is converted into water vapour and removed. This complex process is relatively expensive but helps maintain good flavour which is why it is used with more valuable products such as instant coffee.

What is irradiation?

Irradiation is a method of preservation which uses a carefully controlled dose of radioactive waves called gamma rays to treat and help sterilise foodstuffs.

Gamma rays pass energy through food in a similar way to microwaves, but in irradiation, the food stays cool and bacteria and parasites that can cause diseases in humans are destroyed. Irradiation also kills organisms that cause food to spoil. Despite being passed as safe by the World Health Organisation, the US Food and Drug Administration and a number of other scientific bodies, many consumers have fears about eating food which has been treated with radiation.

Another method of preservation is ultra-heat treated, or UHT. Here, the food is heated to high temperatures which kill bacteria. This can affect the flavour of food.

How big is the food technology industry?

The food industry today is the world's biggest single industry with over £2500 billion spent in 2002. Technology has benefited the food manufacturing industry enormously. It has seen food grown and harvested on an enormous scale through the use of machinery and giant factories built using automation to produce larger quantities of food products at lower cost. Preserving, packaging and storage technologies have made it possible for companies to cut back the amount of food they waste. It also allows them to buy ingredients from and sell their products to countries in every part of the world.

For many companies, sales and profits have soared turning them from small businesses into giant multinational corporations with offices all over the world and sales measured in billions of

When supermarkets first opened, they offered shoppers the chance to buy all of their food produce in one place for the first time.

pounds. Today, the 100 largest food companies in the world account for over 25 per cent of all food products produced. Of those 100 largest companies, around 40 have their headquarters in Europe, 35 are from the United States and 13 are from Japan. Only 12 are from the rest of the world.

How has buying and selling food changed?

Less than a century ago, almost all food shopping was conducted in small stores and markets which served the local community. Both the stores and their customers dealt in small quantities of foods as there was not the technology to store and handle larger amounts. With the rise of new ways of processing and storing foods in factories, shops and homes, food products were increasingly handled in bulk. The first supermarket appeared just over 70 years ago in New York City, and today, small numbers of large supermarket chains dominate food retailing in the more developed nations of Europe and North America. In the UK, for example, 80 per cent of money spent on food went to small shops in 1950. In 2003, the same percentage was spent in just five supermarket chains. These supermarket and food manufacturing giants exert enormous influence on governments as major employers and on the consumer through huge amounts of advertising. They also exert great buying power over their suppliers. Most farmers, for example, are paid lower prices for their crops than in the past and are also pressurised into growing exactly what food industry companies want and at the right times.

Food making in the UK

The food-and-drink manufacturing industry is the single largest manufacturing sector in the UK. Containing over 7700 businesses, the industry employs over 500 000 people and buys two-thirds of all the UK's agricultural produce. Exports of food manufacturing products came to £8.9 billion in 2001.

Source: Food and Drink Federation

The presence of huge food processing plants, such as this fish factory, mean that large amounts of food can be processed and sent to the shops in a very short period of time.

Why Are There Concerns About Food Technology?

There are many concerns about how food technology affects the food we eat including a number of issues surrounding genetically modified foods which are looked at in the next chapter. Many of the other issues are about food safety and the impact of food technology on our health.

THE TYPICAL DIET of people in more developed nations has changed greatly in the past 50 years. Not only do people in wealthier, more developed nations have access to a greater range of individual products, they also have access to an abundant supply of affordable, easy-to-consume foodstuffs. People in these nations today eat large amounts of convenience foods and other heavily processed food products. Many of these products contain high levels of fat and sugar. Studies show that the populations of these countries are

Many people blame the rise in the number of overweight people also on the decline in exercise as people's lives become more sedentary.

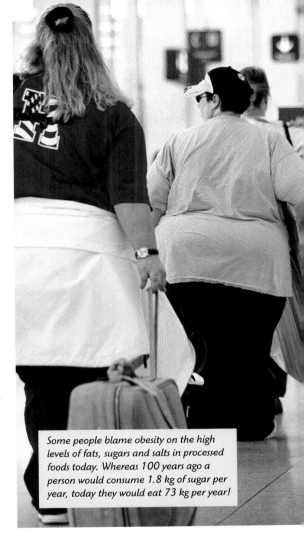

DEBATE - Obesity: is food technology to blame?

- Yes. Food technology has created many convenience foods which are often high in fat and calories – proven causes of obesity. By making such products widely available and cheap, food companies are being irresponsible.

- No. It is the consumer's responsibility to eat a healthy, balanced diet which can include moderate amounts of convenience foods. In addition, there are other factors, such as taking less exercise, which contribute to obesity. Food technology did not create the first high-calorie, high-fat products. Some, such as peanuts, already existed in nature.

Some people blame obesity on the high levels of fats, sugars and salts in processed foods today. Whereas 100 years ago a person would consume 1.8 kg of sugar per year, today they would eat 73 kg per year!

increasingly overweight with many people clinically obese – overweight to the point that they seriously endanger their health. Obesity places a great strain on many of the human body's vital organs and functions. As a result, many people who are severely obese suffer chronic health problems including diabetes, high blood pressure and, in particular, heart problems.

How big a problem is obesity?

The World Health Organisation (WHO) estimates that more than a billion people worldwide are now overweight and that at least 300 million people are considered clinically obese. Numbers are rising sharply. In the United States, direct spending on healthcare due to obesity reached US$70 billion in 2001, around seven per cent of the country's total healthcare budget. In the United States, the Centers For Disease Control and Prevention stated that: 'The most urgent challenge to nutritional health during the 21st century will be obesity.' In the UK, recent studies indicate that one in ten children under the age of four are obese. The International Obesity Taskforce labelled obesity, 'the biggest single European public health challenge of the 21st century.'

Food-borne disease numbers

'More than 200 known diseases are transmitted through food. We estimate that food-borne diseases cause approximately 76 million illnesses, 325 000 hospitalisations and 5000 deaths in the United States each year.'

Source: Food and Drink Federation

How many people are affected by food-borne illnesses?

The WHO estimates that between five and ten per cent of the entire world population suffers from some form of food-borne illness, sometimes called food poisoning, every year. The UK's Food Standards Agency estimates that there are as many as 8.3 million food poisoning cases in the UK every year. Most food poisoning results just in mild sickness, with an upset stomach and nausea. Many cases, however can lead to severe health problems and, in extreme cases, death.

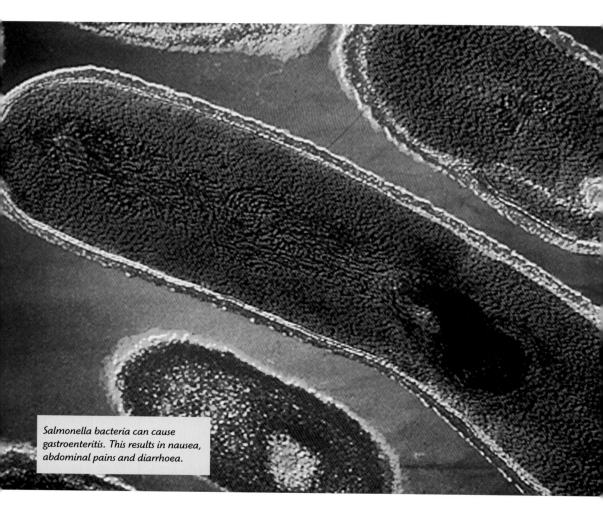

Salmonella bacteria can cause gastroenteritis. This results in nausea, abdominal pains and diarrhoea.

Food poisoning affects millions of people each year. While, for most victims, it means one or two days of sickness, in some cases it can lead to severe illness.

The vast majority of these cases occur due to the presence of toxins or poisons which are produced in food by tiny forms of life called micro-organisms. Not all micro-organisms are harmful, and a number, such as yeast, are actually harnessed in food technology to help create food products as diverse as wine, cheese, bread and yoghurt. However, most incidents of food poisoning are caused by, in particular, bacteria such as *Salmonella, Listeria* and *Campylobacter* in food products. (Details of the seven most common food-borne illness-causing bacteria are found on page 54).

How many cases are caused by food technology?

This is extremely hard for people to estimate. The key cause of most food-borne illnesses is poor hygiene which lets food and food implements become contaminated with bacteria. Poor hygiene can exist in the home and in eating places. On occasion, it has been found to exist in the food industry as well. Critics of modern food technology claim that because food products are manufactured on such a large scale, when food is contaminated it can affect thousands of people over a wide area. Some people feel that with the many stages of manufacture, packing and distribution that a manufactured food product goes through, there is far more potential for contamination problems to occur. They also argue that these many stages make it hard to trace at what point the food became contaminated. For example, in 1994, over 200 000 Americans became ill from eating Schwan's ice cream. After long investigations, it turned out that one of the tanker trucks used to transport the ice cream had previously carried raw eggs contaminated with *Salmonella* bacteria and had not been cleaned or disinfected afterwards.

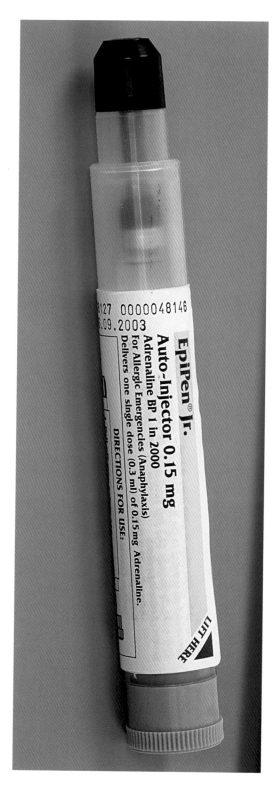

What are food allergies?

Food allergies occur when a person's immune system believes that a harmless food substance is actually harmful. The next time a person eats that food, the immune system releases large amounts of chemicals designed to protect the body. These chemicals can trigger a range of allergic reactions including rashes, hay fever, migraines, asthma and nausea. In more severe cases, victims can suffer breathing problems, a drop in blood pressure, become unconscious and even die. Certain foods, including nuts, milk, wheat and eggs, and some food additives, can be allergens (substances which cause allergic reactions). In the United States alone, some 1.5 million people have an allergy to peanuts which causes between 50 and 100 deaths every year in the USA. Allergy sufferers strive to avoid eating foods containing allergens dangerous to them, but food manufacturing which uses large numbers of ingredients can make this difficult. For example, peanut products such as peanut oil are found in many foods from dips and spaghetti sauces to cakes and ice cream.

Sometimes, they are described on a food label as 'hydrolysed vegetable protein' or 'groundnuts' which are difficult to recognise. There may be errors on labels or ingredients are not identified. Some manufacturers cannot guarantee that their products do not contain allergens due to contamination from another production line or through contamination of raw ingredients. Because of this, companies use phrases like 'may contain' as a warning on their labels.

Many people who suffer severe allergies to nuts or other substances carry an adrenalin kit like this. If they suffer a severe allergic reaction, they can inject themselves with adrenalin which helps to open their airways and blood vessels, reducing the impact of the reaction.

What are food additives?

Additives are substances which are rarely foods themselves but are added to foods to improve the colour, flavour or texture or to help preserve a food's freshness or taste. Emulsifiers, for example, enable fats and oils to mix with water to form smooth textures in products such as margarine. Antioxidants are a type of additive which help prevent fats from turning stale or rancid whilst anti-caking agents ensure powders like flour do not clump together in lumps. E-numbers are a coding system for food additives used in the European Union (EU). For example, E102 is the code for tartrazine, which is frequently used as a colouring.

Special allergy notice: hazelnut alert

'Price Chopper is recalling its bakery four-pack Carrot Muffins packaged at the Niskayuna, NY, store due to undeclared hazelnuts. Due to a printing glitch, hazelnuts are only identified as "ha" on the label.'

Source: Food Allergy & Anaphylaxis Network, 12 May 2003

Some people are allergic to gluten which is found in food made with cereals such as wheat, rye and barley. They must eat gluten-free products, such as rice cakes, honey and yoghurt, which are becoming more widely available.

Why are food additives a big issue?

All food additives in processed foods have to be approved by a country's food safety organisations and strict limits are placed on the amount and type of additives allowed in foods. However, a number of artificial food additives have been directly linked to several health problems including cancer, asthma and hyperactivity in children. Recent cases in the UK involved a number of recalls for food products that were found to contain a potentially dangerous colouring additive called Sudan 1. This dye has been banned in a number of countries after it was shown to cause cancer in laboratory mice. The additive had found its way into a wide range of food products, including herbs and spices used in pasta sauces and ready meals.

Are all food additives artificial?

Not all. While many additives are made artificially, some of the most common additives are natural substances such as lemon juice, salt and sugar. Other food additives are derived from fruits and vegetables. For example, tartaric acid is taken from fruit and is used to make some foods more acidic to improve the length of time they remain edible. Agar, extracted from seaweed, is another additive. It is used as a thickening agent and an emulsifier in many ice creams and some tinned foods.

Is salt bad for us?

People need a small amount of salt (sodium chloride) in their diet to maintain healthy salt levels in the body. Salt has been added to food for centuries

There have been cases of herbs and spices being recalled because they contain the dangerous colour additive, Sudan 1.

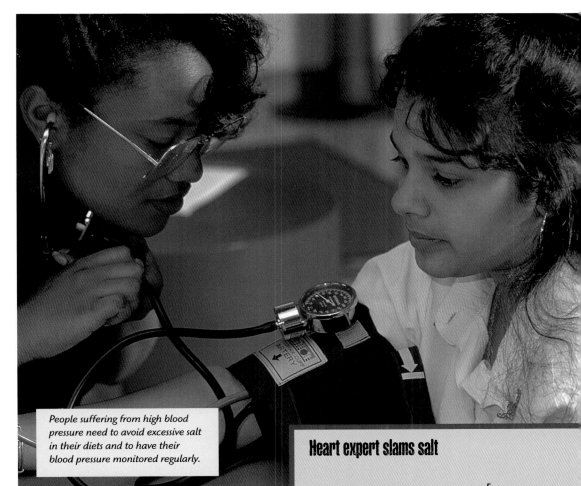

People suffering from high blood pressure need to avoid excessive salt in their diets and to have their blood pressure monitored regularly.

to improve taste and to help preserve foods by killing some bacteria directly as well as drawing water out of the food and depriving other bacteria of the moisture they need.

However, too much salt in a diet can raise blood pressure, a major cause of strokes and heart attacks. It may also contribute to other diseases including asthma. The majority of Americans eat more than double the recommended daily amount of salt. About 80 per cent of the salt they consume is found in processed foods where it is used to give foods flavour, remove chemical aftertastes and reduce dryness.

Heart expert slams salt

'People are much less aware [than in the past] they are eating salt, but it's all hidden in these processed foods. We are talking about foods that are 20–30 per cent more salty than sea water. If we did reduce total salt intake by the recommended amounts, it would save approximately 30 000 heart attacks and strokes in the UK every year.'

Professor Graham McGregor, St George's Hospital, London

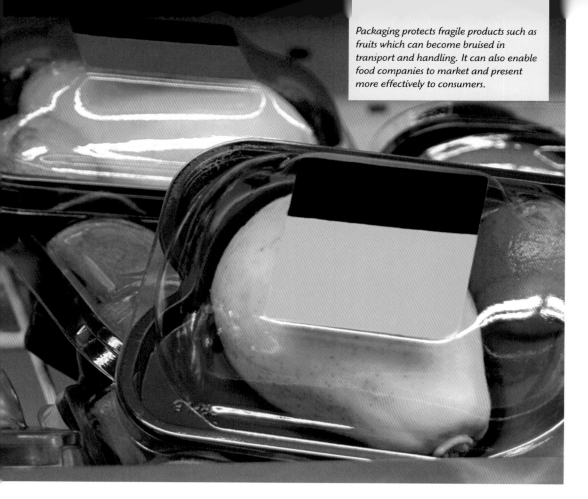

Why are foods packaged?

A century ago, people in many countries would travel to their local store carrying containers which would be filled with milk and loose goods such as flour or sugar. Today, many arrive at their local supermarket by car, ready to fill the boot with large amounts of heavily packaged food products.

Foods are packaged for a variety of different reasons. In some instances, such as canned products, the packaging is essential to the way the food is preserved or it helps promote food safety, as with tamper-proof seals. Other packaging is designed so that foodstuffs can be easily handled, transported and sold by companies. Relatively fragile foods such as fruit, tomatoes, cakes and crackers benefit from protective packaging so that they reach the consumer in perfect condition. Packaging is also used to market and sell food to consumers. Millions of pounds are spent every year by food companies to create packaging which appeals to the consumer, makes the food more convenient to use, makes it appear more attractive and which leads to increases in sales and profits.

Why is packaging a problem?

First and foremost, packaging uses vast amounts of the world's resources. Hundreds of thousands of trees have to be felled to provide paper and cardboard. Millions of litres of oil are used to produce the many types of plastics and foams which form much food packaging. In addition, manufacturing packaging materials uses further resources to generate the large amounts of energy required.

Much food packaging is discarded soon after the food is bought or used and this helps to create the problem of waste. In the United States in 2001, an estimated 190 million tonnes of rubbish was generated, a third of which was packaging. Managing waste is a major ecological problem which uses large areas of land for burying waste in landfill sites and can produce pollution when waste materials are burned.

Other issues surround packaging. Many consumer groups argue that packaging is deliberately designed in order to force people into buying larger quantities of a food than they actually require. Several studies in the USA have shown that food companies provide foods in larger quantities than a typical serving. This can generate waste and it can also encourage people to consume more than they really want.

Large vehicles move around a fraction of the household waste that has been produced by a single town. Much of the solid waste generated is packaging of food items.

A plane sprays pesticide across cropland to eradicate harmful insect pests.

What other concerns exist about food technology?

Many individuals and organisations are concerned about how enormous food manufacturing and retailing companies hold so much power. This power, it is argued, is used to influence governments to prevent new safety measures and higher food standards from becoming law. A pressure group may have funds measured in thousands of pounds to promote their side of an issue. Up against them may be one or more food companies with millions of pounds and influence in government. Many pressure groups believe that giant food companies also use their enormous buying power to exploit farmers and food suppliers, especially those in poorer, less developed nations. Joseph's story at the start of this book is typical of small farmers in many countries.

Other people are concerned with the way that the large-scale farming demanded by massive food companies has major effects on the environment. One example is the massive amounts of pesticides – substances sprayed to destroy insect pests – used in large-scale farming. The pesticides not only remain as a residue on a crop which could affect people's health, but also seep into the soil and through water runoff into streams, rivers and lakes. Over time, a build-up of these poisonous substances can cause major harm to plant and animal life in a region.

Why are people concerned about battery farming?

Many people believe that battery farming is one of a number of farming methods that are cruel to animals.

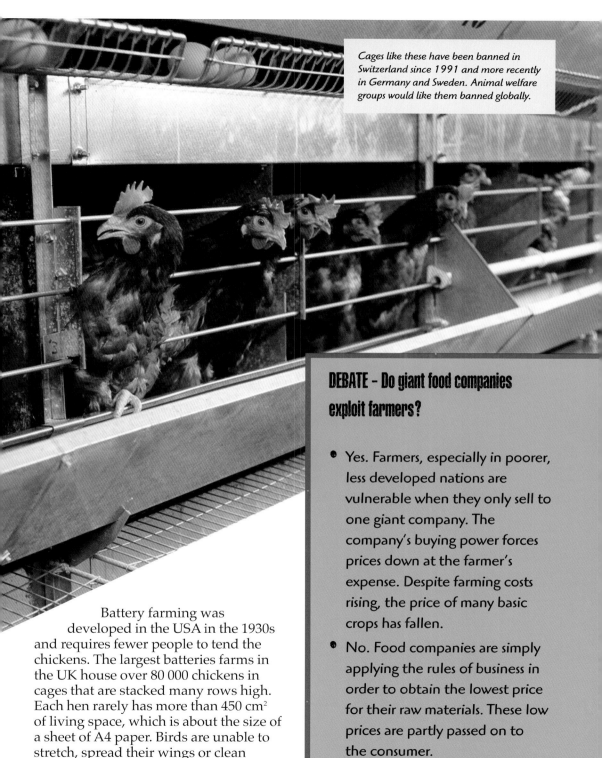

Cages like these have been banned in Switzerland since 1991 and more recently in Germany and Sweden. Animal welfare groups would like them banned globally.

Battery farming was developed in the USA in the 1930s and requires fewer people to tend the chickens. The largest batteries farms in the UK house over 80 000 chickens in cages that are stacked many rows high. Each hen rarely has more than 450 cm² of living space, which is about the size of a sheet of A4 paper. Birds are unable to stretch, spread their wings or clean themselves properly.

DEBATE – Do giant food companies exploit farmers?

- Yes. Farmers, especially in poorer, less developed nations are vulnerable when they only sell to one giant company. The company's buying power forces prices down at the farmer's expense. Despite farming costs rising, the price of many basic crops has fallen.

- No. Food companies are simply applying the rules of business in order to obtain the lowest price for their raw materials. These low prices are partly passed on to the consumer.

What Are Genetically Modified Foods?

Genes are contained in the cells of living things. They guide how living things are made and how they function. After decades of research, scientists have learned how to directly alter the individual genes of many different species of living things in order to create new varieties with desirable characteristics. Much of the research in genetic engineering has been focussed on creating genetically modified (GM) crops and animals for food. The topic of GM foods has aroused large amounts of passionate debate both for and against.

Over the years, apples have been crossed and bred to create the huge number of varieties available today.

ALTERING PLANTS AND animals is not a new innovation. For many centuries, people have been breeding plants and creating hybrids by crossing two similar plants in order to create a new variety. The world's main food crops, such as wheat, barley and potatoes, have all been selected, crossed and bred to suit the conditions they are grown in, to produce greater quantities at harvest time and, sometimes, to make them tastier. The same has occurred with animals. Cattle, for example, have been selectively bred over many centuries to create varieties which yield large quantities of meat or milk. The herds of beef and dairy cattle that exist today vary greatly from each other as well as from cattle which existed thousands of years ago.

A scientist checks on the growth of some genetically modified tomatoes. Several products containing the genetically modified tomatoes have been withdrawn from shops.

How does genetic modification differ from traditional breeding?

Traditional plant and animal breeding involve mixing thousands of genes contained within two plants or animals that are bred or crossed. Genetic modification allows just one or a small number of genes to be altered. Scientists have developed the ability to switch individual genes on or off and they can also insert a gene from a species into a completely different one. For example, scientists have added a gene that is found in the cold-water flounder fish into the genetic make-up of a tomato. The gene makes an anti-freeze chemical enabling the flounder to survive cold conditions. The resulting tomato has been shown to be more frost-resistant than traditional tomatoes.

DNA

Living things are made up of millions of tiny cells, inside each of which is the genetic information which dictates what the living thing will be. This genetic material comes in the form of a long, spiral-shaped molecule called deoxyribonuleic acid (DNA, for short). Scientists have discovered ways to manipulate the DNA directly to create genetically modified plants and animals.

When were the first GM foods sold to the public?

One of the first commercially available GM foods appeared in the United States in 1994. Produced by Calgene, the Flavr Savr tomato was genetically engineered to stay firmer for longer. Tomato soups and puree using GM tomatoes were also introduced.

Where are GM foods grown?

Although many countries are conducting monitored trials of GM crops, just four countries in 2002 grew 99 per cent of the world's commercial GM food crops. These were the USA (66 per cent of world total), Argentina (23 per cent), Canada (6 per cent) and China (4 per cent). A further 11 countries around the world, including Australia, South Africa and Germany, grew much smaller amounts of GM crops. The amount of land devoted to GM crops doubled in the years between 1998 and 2002.

What are the benefits of GM foods?

Those in favour of GM foods maintain that they provide many benefits available both now and in the future. Inserting genes responsible for generating vitamins into crops such as rice and wheat, for example, could increase their nutritional value enormously. Genes added to livestock may make it possible to raise the amount of milk or good quality, low-fat meat they produce. Most GM crops at present are designed to tolerate herbicides (chemicals that kill weeds) allowing farmers to spray to kill weeds without affecting crops. Currently, weeds, along with pests and plant

The growing of GM crops has been carefully monitored to see how they affect the surrounding ecosystem.

DEBATE - Should we oppose the cultivation of GM crops?

- Yes. 'We know there is more than enough food in the world to feed everyone. What is causing world hunger is poverty and inequality. Money would be far better spent tackling these problems than poured into GM technology.'

  Adriano Campolina Soares,
  ActionAid worker, Brazil

- No. 'We can afford to oppose GM crops – our food is already cheap and plentiful. However, in the next 50 years, there will be 3 billion more to feed, mostly in the cities of developing countries... well-fed Westerners have no right to deny others possibilities to improve their lot.'

  Dr Mark Tester, University of Cambridge

Belgian protestors have left this sign after a protest on farmland growing GM crops. The feelings against the growth of GM crops has led to a rise in the number of anti–GM organisations around the globe.

OGM non merci ! oui à la biodiv

diseases, destroy up to one-third of all crops grown. GM crops which are resistant to pests and diseases could cut back much of that waste. By creating GM plants which are resistant to frost, salty soils or drought, land previously difficult to farm could be opened up to produce even more food. Many of those in favour of GM food believe it may provide the answer to feeding a world population which is growing by over 250 000 every day.

Protests against GM crops have included the damaging or destroying of fields hosting GM crop trials.

What GM crops are the most commonly grown?

Maize, cotton and canola make up around 40 per cent of all GM crops grown at present, but the biggest single GM crop is soya beans. Food technologists have learned how to process soya into a variety of forms including soya milk, soya oil and soya protein used as a meat substitute. Soya is also a source of lecithin, found in many foods from sauces to chocolate where it is used as a thickener.

Why are people so against GM foods?

Those against GM foods give a variety of reasons. Some believe that morally we should not be trying to 'play God' and tamper with nature. Others fear for people's jobs and the power that GM companies could hold over the entire food industry. In 2001, 91 per cent of all GM crops grown came from seeds from just one company, Monsanto. GM companies can tie farmers to their products by both developing crops that are only resistant to chemicals they make and by insisting on farmers paying a technology fee to buy GM seeds.

Many fear that once released into the outside world, GM plants could have unforeseen and potentially disastrous effects on the environment. For example, a type of GM corn which produces its own pesticide was believed just to kill pests, but research has shown that it may also kill caterpillars of the harmless Monarch butterfly. Environmental groups are also worried that GM crops

Farm workers in a poor African country have to work hard to grow crops in tough conditions. Many people argue that GM plants will provide crops which are easier to grow, making farmers' lives easier.

could breed with wild plant species. This could, for instance, create weeds resistant to herbicides and thus, uncontrollable. Others fear directly for people's health through eating GM foods. For instance, in the 1990s, US scientists inserted a gene from a Brazil nut into beans to make them more nutritious. But the gene also passed on the property of nuts that causes allergies in people. This was discovered during testing and the project was abandoned.

How Is The Food Industry Regulated?

Every country has laws and agencies designed to ensure that the food their people eat is safe, produced in acceptable ways and reaches the standards set. However, many examples of bad practice in the food industry still occur and these have helped prompt the rise of many pressure groups. They strive to make the public aware of food technology issues and campaign to make food safer for the public.

FOOD MANUFACTURERS spend millions of pounds every year on food hygiene and safety. Many companies use a system called Hazard Analysis and Critical Control Points (HACCP). This identifies the key stages in a food product's production where food hazards can occur so that measures can be introduced to monitor quality and check for risks. The food that is sold to people in more developed nations is also governed by many laws which are enforced by hygiene and food safety inspectors and agencies. In the UK, for instance, Environmental Health Officers (EHOs) visit food industry factories and

This food inspector is testing the quality and safety of coffee beans.

Leading executives from Japan's largest dairy company, Snow Brand, announced that the company would disband after a series of food safety incidents triggered a boycott by shops.

retail outlets investigating complaints and checking on levels of hygiene and safe storage. Failure to reach standards can lead to court cases, fines and products being banned.

However, many believe that food companies get away with thousands of illegal practices or, if caught, are punished too lightly. Critics argue that compared to the millions of pounds large food companies make every day, a fine of a few thousand pounds will have little impact. In 2003, new food safety laws were proposed for the countries of the European Union (EU) which were far stricter than before. These laws proposed that farmers and food retailers could be jailed or have their businesses shut down if they broke new laws on, for example, trying to sell food with banned or unsafe levels of additives or pesticides. Making these new proposals law is one thing, but managing to enforce them is quite another.

Mad Cow Disease

Bovine spongiform encephalopathy (BSE) is a disease that affects adult cattle, attacking the brain and central nervous system of the animal and eventually causing death. Many scientists believe that there are links between BSE and a serious human disease known as Creutzfeldt-Jakob Disease (CJD). Outbreaks of BSE throughout much of the 1990s saw the UK cattle industry devastated. More than 4.6 million older British cows were slaughtered to prevent the disease spreading. New laws mean that only cattle under the age of 30 months can be used as food. Feeding any farm animal with material that includes processed body parts of sheep or cattle is now banned in the UK as this is believed to have been one of the causes of the disease's spread.

The wide range of foodstuffs on supermarket shelves gives an indication of the number of products created by the food industry.

Why is monitoring food safety so difficult?

There are tens of thousands of food products available to consumers with many more being introduced every year. Each product can use many ingredients and many different processes in its manufacture. In addition, an individual food product may be produced in a number of different locations, in different batches and sent to different markets. Trying to keep track of all the foods, ingredients, additives and processes used to make them involves a vast amount of work.

Food hygiene, safety and health agencies in many countries are simply overwhelmed with work and often do not have the staff or funding to investigate all these foodstuffs or visit the many thousands of food factories, distributors and retailers that exist. In addition, the food standards and laws in different countries can vary greatly, making the tracing of food ingredients from overseas especially difficult.

Because food from one source can be distributed all over a large country or, further still, to many different countries, outbreaks of an illness can appear to be unrelated. In 1998, some 100 cases of *Listeria* which caused 22 deaths in the USA appeared to be unrelated but through investigations, they were traced to hot dogs and sliced meats manufactured by one factory. Food agencies in many wealthier countries are starting to use information technology to communicate food safety issues and to trace food problems back to their source. For example, the United States has established PulseNet, a computer network linking public health laboratories all over the country. It acts as an early warning system for outbreaks of food-borne disease.

Why is there a need for more scientific research?

Our knowledge of food and health is far from complete. For example, we do not yet know the full extent of the effect of some modern food additives on the human body over a long period of time. Nor do we fully know the effects on people or the environment of intensive farming and eating of GM food. Every year, new food technology techniques and many new products reach the market. Whilst some testing is performed on these new foods and techniques to gain approval, many experts believe that not enough long term studies are being conducted to measure the effects of modern food on people's health.

Hot dogs and other processed meat products such as burgers can often cause food poisoning due to their poor preparation, heating and serving at some fast food stalls and outlets.

Another successful campaign saw the introduction of restrictions on the transport of live animals around the UK. Many people were concerned that the animals were being made to suffer unnecessarily.

Who campaigns for consumers and have they been successful?

Dozens of campaign and pressure groups exist in countries and many are growing in strength due to large numbers of people losing confidence in the safety and standards of food. Many groups have campaigned heavily in Europe against GM foods. Although there are crop trial sites, no GM crops are currently commercially grown in the UK or in a number of other European Union nations. There have been other successes. For example, following public pressure, battery cages for egg-laying chickens were banned in Switzerland in 1991 and more recently in Germany and Sweden. In the UK, after it was

highlighted by a number of consumer groups, the bleaching of flour to make it whiter using a chemical called benzoyl peroxide was banned in 1997. However, the chemical is still widely used in many other countries.

Why is labelling important?

Labels are designed to allow consumers to know what is contained within the food they are buying so that a customer can make a decision based on its ingredients. Some consumers may wish to choose a foodstuff which does not contain a specific ingredient for health or other reasons. In the form of 'use by' or 'sell by' dates, labels can also offer assistance in food safety. However, many food safety pressure groups are concerned that labelling laws in many countries are not strict enough. In many cases, they argue, labels are unclear, misleading or not completely accurate. For example, in Europe, all foods containing GM ingredients must be labelled so that shoppers know what they are buying. However small amounts below one per cent of GM material in foods need not be labelled at the current time. In the UK, a number of unwrapped foods such as breads, foods from a cooked food counter or sweets do not have to carry ingredient lists but any main additives must be publicly displayed on a ticket or notice nearby. In practice, this is not always done.

DEBATE – Should there be more labelling information?

- Yes. The consumer has a fundamental right to know exactly what they are buying and eating right down to the smallest quantity of ingredient. 100 per cent accurate labelling would force food manufacturers to trace every element of their food production process.

- No. Further food information would confuse the public. Even if listed, most people would not recognise the names of chemical additives or understand what they are. Labelling every single ingredient might be difficult and expensive for manufacturers who would have to pass the cost on to consumers.

Food labels may carry a lot of information, including the contents of the food, how best to store it and even serving suggestions. Some people feel that adding more details would only confuse consumers.

What Is The Future For Food Technology?

No one can predict with certainty what the future holds for food technology and the food industry, but some trends are likely to continue for many years to come. Among these are further demands from many consumers for greater choice, lower prices and foods which fit in with their lifestyle. Food safety, hygiene, how foods are produced and what ingredients and additives they contain are also likely to become bigger public issues.

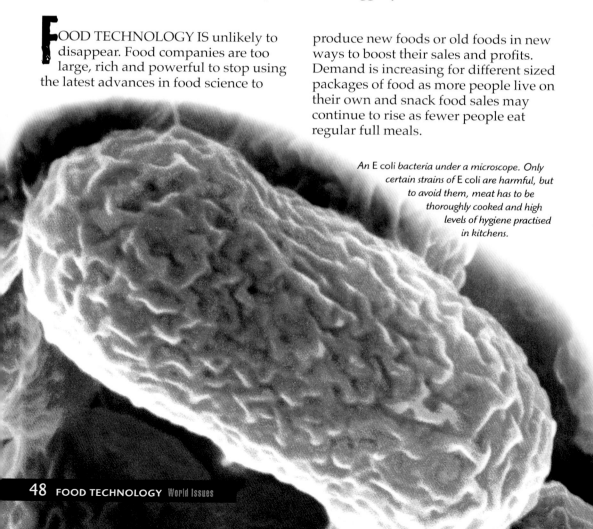

FOOD TECHNOLOGY IS unlikely to disappear. Food companies are too large, rich and powerful to stop using the latest advances in food science to produce new foods or old foods in new ways to boost their sales and profits. Demand is increasing for different sized packages of food as more people live on their own and snack food sales may continue to rise as fewer people eat regular full meals.

An E coli bacteria under a microscope. Only certain strains of E coli are harmful, but to avoid them, meat has to be thoroughly cooked and high levels of hygiene practised in kitchens.

Government officers burn carcasses of dead cows during the foot–and–mouth outbreak which took hold in the UK.

Why may food safety become a bigger issue?

People are becoming increasingly informed about the food they eat, their nutritional requirements and their diet. Major issues, such as the BSE crisis and the foot-and-mouth outbreak, as well as the debate on genetically modified foods have raised the public's awareness of issues about food in general. At the same time, the populations of many of the world's developed nations are becoming increasingly old and increasingly overweight on average, while more money is being spent by health organisations in these countries to promote information about eating well and staying healthy.

New safety technology is likely to be introduced for many foods. For example, a Canadian company, Toxin Alert, has recently invented a plastic wrapper coated with chemicals which change colour if they come into contact with a number of food-borne illness-causing bacteria including *Salmonella* and *E Coli*. On the other hand, many campaign groups believe that it will take more than extra technology to stem the large number of food-borne illnesses that occur. They believe that far stricter laws on food safety and hygiene and greater punishments for those that break the laws, will be required if food is to become safer.

Organic farming not only seeks to produce healthy food but also to create farming systems where animal welfare and care of the environment are priorities.

What are organic foods?

Alternatives to intensively farmed foods using large amounts of chemicals and processing do exist particularly in the form of organic foods. Organic farms may still use high-tech equipment such as mechanised harvesters but they avoid the use of chemical pesticides and fertilisers. Supporters of organic farming maintain that the food produced is healthier and the farm soil is kept in better condition. Food that is organically grown is frequently more expensive because it is not produced in such large quantities as crops grown on large-scale farms. However, if organic farming was practised on a larger scale, the price gap between factory farmed and organic farmed produce would shrink greatly. Some three per cent of all food bought in the UK, for instance, is organic produce. This may rise greatly in the future.

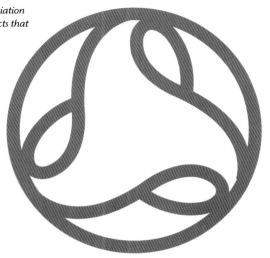

The logo of the UK's Soil Association which appears on food products that meet its standards.

There are also several organisations that have been established to monitor the production of organic food. In the UK, for example, the Soil Association oversees standards for the whole organic food industry. Its logo only appears on food that has been produced according to rigorous standards. Products bearing this logo are designed to offer consumers safe, nourishing food from healthy plants and animals.

What will the future bring for GM foods?

Much depends on what advances are made and whether GM crops are accepted by governments and consumers worldwide, but GM foods may have a major role in the food of the future. Crops which generate their own pesticides could reduce farming's reliance on harmful chemicals. Foods may be grown which manufacture large amounts of vitamins and other nutrients which people need for a healthy diet. For example, GM golden rice, is being developed for Asia, the home of 90 per cent of the world's grown rice. This rice is rich in the building blocks of vitamin A. Deficiency in this vitamin can cause blindness and other diseases. The future may also see GM animals and plants turned into biological factories which produce incredibly useful substances such as vaccines for diseases or biofuels which may power motor vehicles. Opponents of GM foods believe that their impact on the food supply may not be so large either because GM foods will remain unpopular with consumers or a major environmental scare may prevent their further development.

The decaffeinated coffee plant

Caffeine is a drug found in coffee which can increase blood pressure and be harmful. Taking the caffeine out to create decaffeinated coffee is an expensive process. Japanese genetic engineers at the Nara Institute of Science and Technology have produced GM coffee plants which contain only 30 per cent of the caffeine found in normal plants. They managed to switch off one of the genes responsible for generating much of the caffeine found in coffee. The future could see far cheaper and healthier decaffeinated coffee produced naturally.

Source: New Scientist, 2003

REFERENCE

25 LARGEST FOOD MANUFACTURING COMPANIES IN THE WORLD (BY FOOD SALES IN MILLIONS OF US DOLLARS)

Company (Country of Headquarters)	Sales	Products
1 Nestlé SA (Switzerland)	$46 628	Various
2 Kraft Foods Inc (USA)	$38 119	Various
3 ConAgra Inc (USA)	$27 630	Various
4 PepsiCo Inc (USA)	$26 935	Beverages and snack foods
5 Unilever plc (UK/the Netherlands)	$26 672	Various
6 Archer Daniels Midland Co (USA)	$23 454	Ingredients, cereal products
7 Cargill Inc (USA)	$21 500	Grain-based foods
8 The Coca-Cola Co (USA)	$20 092	Beverages
9 Diageo plc (UK)	$16 644	Alcoholic beverages
10 Mars Inc (USA)	$15 300	Confectionery
11 Anheuser-Busch Inc (USA)	$12 262	Brewery
12 Groupe Danone (France)	$12 184	Dairy, biscuits, water
13 Kirin Brewery Co Ltd (Japan)	$11 287	Beverages
14 Asahi Breweries Ltd (Japan)	$11 050	Brewery
15 Tyson Foods (USA)	$10 751	Meat and poultry
16 Dean Foods Co (USA)	$9700	Dairy
17 HJ Heinz Co (USA)	$9431	Frozen and shelf-stable foods
18 Sara Lee Corp (USA)	$9219	Meats, bakery, beverages
19 Kellogg Co (USA)	$8853	Grain-based foods
20 Snow Brand Milk (Japan)*	$8511	Dairy
21 Heineken NV (the Netherlands)	$8233	Brewery
22 Cadbury Schweppes plc (UK)	$8070	Beverages, confections
23 General Mills Inc (USA)	$7949	Grain-based foods
24 Dairy Farmers (USA)	$7902	Dairy
25 Nippon Meat Packers Inc (Japan)	$7589	Meat processor

*Snow Brand in the process of merging with Nestlé SA

Source: *Food Engineering Magazine*, 2002

TOP TEN GLOBAL FOOD RETAILERS, 2002

Company (Country of Headquarters)	Number of Stores	Sales in US Dollars
1 Wal-Mart Stores (USA) *Argentina, Brazil, Canada, China, Germany, Japan, Mexico, Singapore, South Korea, United Kingdom, USA, Vietnam	5164	$244.5 billion
2 Carrefour (France) *Argentina, Belgium, Brazil, Chile, China, Colombia, Czech Republic, Dominican Republic, Egypt, France, Greece, Indonesia, Italy, Japan, Malaysia, Mexico, Oman, Poland, Portugal, Qatar, Romania, Singapore, Slovakia, South Korea, Spain, Switzerland, Taiwan, Thailand, Tunisia, Turkey, USA	10 704	$64.7 billion
3 Ahold (Netherlands) *Argentina, Brazil, Chile, Costa Rica, Czech Republic, Denmark, Ecuador, El Salvador, Estonia, Guatemala, Honduras, Indonesia, Latvia, Lithuania, Malaysia, Netherlands, Nicaragua, Norway, Paraguay, Peru, Poland, Portugal, Slovakia, Spain, Sweden, Thailand, USA	9407	$59.2 billion
4 Kroger (USA) *USA	3667	$51.8 billion
5 Metro (Germany) *Austria, Belgium, Bulgaria, China, Croatia, Czech Republic, Denmark, France, Germany, Greece, Hungary, India, Italy, Japan, Luxembourg, Morocco, Netherlands, Poland, Portugal, Romania, Russia, Slovakia, Spain, Switzerland, Turkey, United Kingdom, Ukraine, Vietnam	2411	$48.5 billion
6 Tesco (UK) *Czech Republic, Hungary, Ireland, Malaysia, Poland, Slovakia, South Korea, Taiwan, Thailand, United Kingdom, USA	2294	$39.5 billion
7 Costco (USA) *Canada, Japan, Mexico, South Korea, Taiwan, United Kingdom, USA	400	$38 billion
8 Albertsons (USA) *USA	1688	$35.6 billion
9 Rewe Zentrale (Germany) *Austria, Bulgaria, Croatia, Czech Republic, France, Germany, Hungary, Italy, Poland, Romania, Slovakia, Ukraine	12 077	$35.2 billion
10 Aldi (Germany) *Australia, Austria, Belgium, Denmark, France, Germany, Ireland, Luxembourg, Netherlands, Spain, United Kingdom, USA	6609	$33.7 billion

*Indicates countries of operation

Source: *Supermarket News, 2002, M+M Planet Retail, 2002*

BACTERIA FACTFILE

SEVEN TYPES OF BACTERIA ARE RESPONSIBLE FOR THE MAJORITY OF THE REPORTED CASES OF FOOD-BORNE ILLNESS.

Salmonella species

The *Salmonella* family includes about 2000 different strains of bacteria, but only ten strains cause most of the reported *Salmonella* infections. *Salmonella* can be found in a variety of sources particularly chickens and other poultry, meat, eggs and unpasteurised milk. Improperly cooked foods are a common cause of infections.

Campylobacter jejuni

Campylobacter is the most commonly identified cause of food-borne disease. It has been found mainly in poultry, red meat, unpasteurised milk and untreated water. Common symptoms include diarrhoea, fever and abdominal pains.

E coli

E coli is a bacterium that normally lives in the intestines of people and animals. Most types of *E coli* are harmless. However, one type, called *E coli* 0157:H7, can produce a deadly toxin and can cause illness, with children and old people the most vulnerable. Sources include meat, especially undercooked minced beef, milk and milk produce.

Staphylococcus aureus

These bacteria are carried by humans in their noses and throats as well as in skin infections. Ordinary cooking does not kill the toxin produced by *Staphylococcus* bacteria, which is why personal hygiene is so important in the kitchen. Cooked meats, sandwiches and products containing cream which have been handled in non-hygienic conditions are common sources of *Staphylococcus*.

Clostridium perfringens

These are bacteria present throughout the environment, growing where there is little or no oxygen. Illness, which can cause dehydration, cramps and diarrhoea, comes when consuming food which is contaminated by large numbers of *Clostridium perfringens*. Foods, especially meats, in buffets, casseroles, stews and gravies where the temperature is not kept above 60°C are the most susceptible.

Clostridium botulinum

This bacteria can produce a toxic substance which causes botulism, a severe illness. Cases of botulism are rare but very dangerous with blurred vision and breathing difficulties and, in some cases, paralysis and death. Foods at risk are those which have been improperly processed or stored such as dented canned foods.

Listeria monocytogenes

The cause of the disease listeriosis, *Listeria* bacteria survive at temperatures below zero and grow best between 0°C and 5°C, the temperature range that we use for refrigeration. The bacteria can be found in milk, raw vegetables, soft or semi-soft cheese, pâté, meat and poultry.

TOTAL AREA IN MILLIONS OF HECTARES GROWN WITH GM CROPS (1996–2002)

Crop	1996	1997	1998	1999	2000	2001	2002 (mha)
Soybean	0.5	5.1	14.5	21.6	25.8	33.3	36.5
Corn	0.3	3.2	8.3	11.1	10.3	9.8	12.4
Cotton	0.8	1.4	2.5	3.7	5.3	6.8	6.8
Canola	0.1	1.2	2.4	3.4	2.8	2.7	3.0
Potato	0.1	0.1	0.1	0.1	0.1	0.1	0
Tobacco	1.0	1.6	0	0	0	0	0
Tomato	0.1	0.1	0	0	0	0	0
Squash	0	0	0	0.1	0.1	0.1	0.1
Papaya	0	0	0	0.1	0.1	0.1	0.1
Total	2.8	12.8	27.8	39.9	44.2	52.6	58.7

Source: ISAAA, Global Knowledge Centre

PERCENTAGE OF UNDERNOURISHED PEOPLE IN POPULATION (SELECTED COUNTRIES)

Country

Country		Country	
Congo DR	73%	Papua New Guinea	27%
Somalia	71%	Guatemala	25%
Afghanistan	70%	India	24%
Burundi	69%	Bolivia	23%
Eritrea	58%	Venezuela	21%
Mozambique	55%	Croatia	18%
Haiti	50%	Bulgaria	15%
Sierra Leone	47%	Cuba	13%
Mongolia	42%	Jamaica	9%
Cambodia	36%	China	9%
Bangladesh	35%	Indonesia	6%
Nicaragua	29%	Mexico	5%
Iraq	27%		

Source: UN FAO State Of Food Insecurity In The World, 2002

While almost everyone can afford basic food in wealthier, more developed nations, a lack of basic food leading to malnutrition is a major problem affecting peoples in many nations. The countries above have been selected to highlight how the problem of malnutrition occurs on every continent.

GLOSSARY

additives Substances added to food to aid processing, preservation or to improve flavour or colour.

aquaculture The farming of freshwater and saltwater species including fish, shellfish and seaweed.

bacteria A large group of different types of single-celled micro-organisms, some of which are harmful and some of which are helpful in food and food technology.

biodiversity Short for biological diversity, the range of species of living things. The greater the biodiversity of an area, the greater the number of species it contains.

biotechnology The use of living things to make or change products including food.

BSE (Bovine spongiform encephalopathy) Nicknamed 'mad cow disease' and believed to be transmitted between different animal species due to the use of animal products in animal feed.

consumer A person who uses goods and services.

contamination A process by which harmful or unpleasant substances (such as odours, bacteria or poisons) get into or onto food.

DNA Short for deoxyribonucleic acid, it is found inside a living cell and carries the information living things require to function, repair and reproduce.

emulsifiers Substances which allow the mixing of two or more liquids that normally do not mix together well. They work by coating the surface of droplets of one liquid in such a way that they can stay dispersed in the second liquid.

enzymes Chemical substances that speed up chemical reactions.

fermentation The process by which sugar and starches are turned into alcohol to produce wine and beer. This process is achieved with the aid of micro-organisms, such as yeast.

food-borne illness A disease that is carried or transmitted to humans by food containing harmful substances. Examples are the disease salmonellosis, which is caused by *Salmonella* bacteria.

food irradiation A method of preserving foods using a form of radiation.

food processing Using food as a raw material and changing it in some way to make a food product.

genes Consisting of DNA, they carry the instructions for all the characteristics or traits which a living thing inherits.

genetically modified foods Any food containing parts of genetically modified plants, animals or micro-organisms.

heat sealing A method of sealing plastic containers by heating two layers or portions of the container until they melt together to form a good seal.

herbicide A substance used as a weed killer when growing crops.

hermetic The sealing of a package so that it cannot let in micro-organisms, water, gas or dust to contaminate the food inside.

homogenise The process in which milk is forced through tiny holes to break up fats so that they are distributed evenly throughout the milk.

HACCP Short for Hazard Analysis Critical Control Point, it is a system used in the food industry to ensure that safety is maintained at all points in its production.

irrigation A human-made system of watering the land using pipes and ditches to channel water.

micro-organisms Living things which are very small, can usually only be seen under a microscope and, in some cases, may cause disease.

moulds A group of fungi which grow in thread-like strands called hyphae. Moulds can grow on foods and damage them but some are introduced into foods to give added flavour, for example, in some cheeses such as Stilton.

organic farming Food produced without the use of synthetic chemicals and with concern for the environment.

outbreak An incident in which two or more people experience the same illness after eating the same food.

pasteurisation A process designed to destroy harmful bacteria in liquid foods, such as milk, by using high temperatures.

perishable A food that spoils quickly and needs careful storage.

pesticide A chemical substance which is poisonous to particular insect pests. Pesticides are usually sprayed onto crops to prevent damage by pests.

pollution Waste products or heat which damages the environment in some way.

preservation Any process used to slow or stop the progress of foods spoiling.

processing Treating a food in such a way as to change its nature and properties in order to preserve it, to improve its eating quality or to make useful ingredients.

retailer The seller of goods or services to the consumer for personal use.

runoff The part of rainfall which reaches streams or rivers. The remainder either evaporates back into the atmosphere or seeps below ground.

shelf life The expected length of time a food will maintain its best quality.

species A set of organisms which can be grouped together due to their similarity and their potential ability to breed with each other.

sterilisation A process in which foods are treated to kill all forms of micro-organisms. Foods can be sterilised with high temperatures or using radiation.

tamper-proof seals Devices attached to food packages that indicate if a package has been opened or not.

toxic Any substance which is poisonous or harmful to life.

UHT Short for ultra-heat treated, a method of preserving certain foods such as soups, sauces, milk and milk products, by exposing the food to a very high temperature for a short period of time.

vacuum A place or region containing no solid, liquid or gas.

value-added The processing of products so that their selling price is higher than that of the raw materials from which they were made.

FURTHER INFORMATION

BOOKS and MAGAZINES

World Issues: Genetic Engineering,
Steve Parker, Belitha Press 2002

Food Technology: An Introduction,
Anita Tull, Oxford University Press 2002
A clearly written overview of aspects of
the food industry.

Food Technology, Mark Lambert,
Wayland 1991
A history of food technology and
overview of many of the key ways foods
are processed and preserved.

*Eat Your Genes: How Genetically Modified
Food Is Entering Our Diet*,
Stephen Nottingham, Zed Books 1999
An in-depth look at how genetic
modification developed, its benefits and
the concerns that people have.

Healthy Eating Issues, Edited by Craig
Donnellan, Independence Educational
Publishers 2001
A resources book containing reports,
newspaper articles and surveys from
government, industry and pressure
groups about food, food technology
and nutrition.

Trends In Food Technology: Safe Food,
Hazel King, Heinemann 2003
An example-based guide to the risks in
food and the hygiene and caring
systems used in factories, distribution
and kitchens.

Biotechnology Unzipped, Eric S Grace,
Joseph Henry Press 1997
A clear and detailed account of the rise of
biotechnology and how it has affected
many foods, how they are processed and
the impact on stores and customers.

ORGANISATIONS

British Nutrition Foundation
High Holborn House
52–54 High Holborn
London
WC1V 6RQ
United Kingdom
http://www.nutrition.org.uk

European Food Information Council
19, rue Guimard
1040 Brussels
Belgium
Tel: +32 2 506 89 89
Fax: +32 2 506 89 80
http://www.eufic.org

US Food and Drug Administration
5600 Fishers Lane
Rockville
MD 20857-0001
USA
Tel: +1 888 463 6332
http://www.fda.gov/

Food Standards Agency Helpline
Room 245, Aviation House
125 Kingsway
London WC2B 6NH
Tel: 020 7276 8000
Fax: 020 7238 6330
http://www.food.gov.uk

Institute of Food Technologists
525 West Van Buren, Suite 1000
Chicago
IL 60607
USA
Tel: +1 312 782 8424
Fax: +1 312 782 8348

Institute of Food Science & Technology
5 Cambridge Court
210 Shepherd's Bush Road
London W6 7NJ
Tel: 020 7603 6316
Fax: 020 7602 9936
http://www.ifst.org

Centre for Food Technology
Agency for Food and Fibre Sciences
19 Hercules St
Hamilton
Queensland
Australia 4007
Tel: +61 (0)7 3406 8555
Fax: +61 (0)7 3406 8665
Email: cft@dpi.qld.gov.au

World Health Organisation
Avenue Appia 20
1211 Geneva 27
Switzerland
Tel: +41 22 791 21 11
Fax: +41 22 791 31 11

WEBSITES

http://www.foodsafety.gov/
A gateway to many reports and
frequently asked questions about food
technology and food safety in the
United States.

http:www.fao.org
The home on the Internet of the United
Nations Food and Agriculture
Organisation (FAO). One of the largest
organisations within the United
Nations, the FAO's website contains
hundreds of webpages of statistics,
articles and reports.

www.monsanto.com
One of the largest companies involved in
biotechnology and genetic modification,
Monsanto's home website, based in the
United States, contains details of the
company's products and research.

http://www.gmnation.org.uk/
This is the official website for the Genetic
Modification (GM) public debate which
took place in the United Kingdom in
June, 2003. The website contains articles
and opinions from all viewpoints.

http://www.ift.org/
The homepage of the Institute of Food
Technologists contains a wealth of
information including back issues of
Food Technology magazine online.

http://www.foodtech.org.uk/
A website designed for pupils and
teachers interested in learning more
about food processing and packaging
in industry.

http://www.nal.usda.gov/fsrio/
Homepage of the American Food Safety
Research Information Office with dozens
of links to issues concerning food safety,
food technology and the food industry
in general.

http://www.foodhaccp.com/education
A large collection of hyperlinks to
websites concerned with food
technology and food safety.

INDEX

irradiation 20, 21, 56
Italy 19

Japan 9, 22, 43, 51

Kenya 8

labels 28, 46, 47
landfill sites 33
lecithin 40
lemon juice 30
Listeria 27, 45, 54
lyophilisation 20

maize 14, 40
margarine 29
meats 14, 15, 36, 38, 48, 54
micro-organisms 14, 15,
   27, 56, 57
microwave ovens 10, 17
Middle East 13
milk 9, 12, 15, 16, 28, 32,
   36, 38, 54
   pasteurised 12
Monsanto 40

Nara Institute of Science
   and Technology 51
nausea 26, 28
New York 15, 23
nuts 28, 41
   Brazil nuts 41
   groundnuts 29
   hazelnuts 29

obesity 25
oils 29, 32
organic foods 50, 51

Pacific Ocean 18
packaging 8, 14, 22, 32, 33
parasites 21
pasta 19, 20
Pasteur, Louis 15
pasteurisation 15, 16, 20,
   57

peaches 34
peanuts 25, 28
   peanut oil 28
pesticides 8, 34, 40, 50, 57
pests 34, 38, 39, 40
plastics 12, 14, 20, 33
popcorn 12
potatoes 36, 55
pressure groups 34, 42, 46
processing plants 9, 23
proteins 28
protests 39, 40
PulseNet 45

Quorn 19

radiation 11
rashes 28
ready meals 11, 16, 17, 19,
   30
rice 20, 38
   golden rice 51
   rice cakes 29
runoff 34, 57
rye 29

Salmonella 26, 27, 49, 54,
   56
salt 17, 30, 31
sauces 30, 40
sausages 19
Schwan 27
seaweed 30
seeds 13, 40
sheep 43
Snow Brand 9, 43, 52
Soil Association 51
South Africa 38
soya 19
   beans 40
   milk 40
   oil 40
   protein 40
spices 30
storage 22, 43
strawberries 11

sugar 13, 24, 30, 32
supermarkets 12, 18, 22,
   23, 37, 44
Sweden 35, 46
sweet peppers 34
Switzerland 35, 46

tamper-proof seals 32, 57
tartaric acid 30
tartrazine 29
Thai food 19
thickening agents 30, 40
tofu 19
tomatoes 32, 37, 55
   Flavr Savr 38
Toxin Alert 49
toxins 27
transportation 16, 32, 46
tuberculosis 16
typhoid 16

UK 9, 23, 25, 26, 30, 35, 43,
   46, 47, 49, 50
ultra-heat treated (UHT)
   21, 57
USA 9, 10, 19, 22, 25, 28,
   33, 35, 38, 45
US Food and Drug
   Administration 21, 34,
   44

vacuum-sealing 20
vegetables 9, 14, 15, 30
vitamins 38, 51

waste 16, 33, 39
water 20, 29, 31
weeds 38, 41
wheat 13, 14, 28, 29, 36, 38
wine 15, 27
World Health
   Organisation (WHO) 21,
   25, 26

yeasts 13, 27
yoghurt 27, 29